50 WAYS TO PLAY YOUR RHYTHMIC PHRASE

BY JOHN LEZANA

FREE MP3 DOWNLOADS AVAILABLE AT WWW.SOUNDCLOUD.COM/JOHN-LEZANA

50 WAYS TO PLAY YOUR RHYTHMIC PHRASE © JOHN LEZANA 2012.
ACKNOWLEDGEMENTS: BASS / PAUL COOK, GUITAR / ELLIOT COOMBS

ALL RIGHTS OF THE PRODUCER/OWNER REPRODUCED RESERVED. UNAUTHORISED COPYING, HIRING, RENTING, PUBLIC PERFORMANCES AND BROADCASTING OF MATERIAL AND RECORDINGS PROHIBITED.
PUBLISHED BY JOHN LEZANA   DESIGN: NICOLA PLUMB

INTRODUCTION

"50 ways to play your rhythmic phrase" has been in my head for many years and has helped me to develop not only my phrasing ideas but also my grooves and technique. In fact, it has helped me with all aspects of my drumming including sight reading and transcribing.

I use a lot of these ideas in my playing and also my teaching. I now believe this is the right time to categorise some of the more useful ideas used in everyday drumming and place them in a book format for others to read, learn from and develop their own ideas.

The concept of taking one rhythmic phrase and using it in many different ways is not new. The written word provides the reader and student drummer with a workable and useful model with which to learn from and make their own.

Ideally, the student should seek to get the rhythmic phrases into muscle memory. Muscle memory will ensure that any learnt rhythmic phrases are easily recalled at will, when needed. This is largely achieved by practice, practice, practice thus perfecting them over time.

Remember, all good things come to those who wait, meaning some of the examples in this book will take longer than others to learn and perfect. Use a click at 60 b.p.m to start with and try to explore different orchestrations within each example. This will help you develop it into something that you know and feel is right for you.

Playing and learning the drums is a lifelong process. New techniques coupled with consistent/regular practice will lead to much improvement and a greater satisfaction. You will achieve your goals.

The mindset of, "I can't do it" is not an option. Practice, practice, practice and you will succeed. It's a "can do" mindset that will help you achieve your goals.

Oh and yes, remember to have FUN! That's probably the reason you started drumming in the first place.

Good luck and happy drumming.

John Lezana

DRUM KIT NOTATION KEY

The following system of drum kit notation is employed in this book

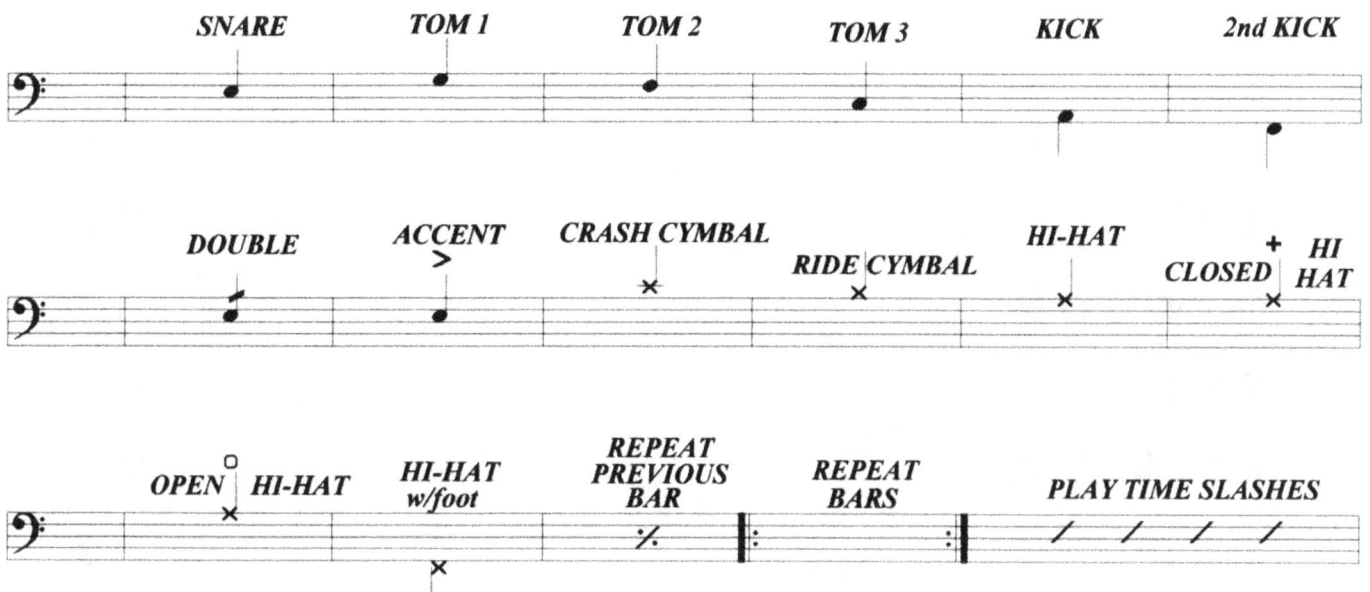

CONTENTS

The Rhythmic Phrase	4
Examples 1-10	4-6
Solo 1	7-8
Examples 11-20	9-10
Solo 2	11-12
Examples 21-30	13-15
Solo 3	16-17
Examples 31-40	18-20
Solo 4	21-22
Examples 41-50	23-25
Solo 5	26-27
50 Bonus ideas No.1-19	28-31
Phrase permutations No.20-35	32-33
4 ideas to apply to phrase permutations	34
Groove ideas No.40-44	35
Metric modulation No.45-50	36-37
Use for your own ideas	38-39

THE RHYTHMIC PHRASE

The rhythmic phrase is very common in one form or another in all styles of music. You will learn to recognise patterns that crop up in music over and over again by practicing them and exploring different ways of playing them.

This common phrase has notes on beat 1, a of 1, & of 2, e of 3, 4 and the & of 4.

EXAMPLE 1

Taking the phrase and accenting it through 16th notes on the snare with ¼ notes in the left foot/ Hi-hat foot to keep time. Start slowly with a click or metronome at 60 b.p.m (beats per minute) on all examples. When you feel comfortable that the pattern sounds smooth with nice dynamics and in time, increase the tempo.

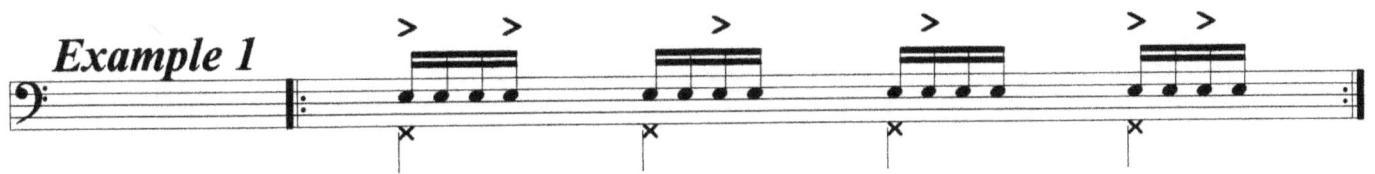

EXAMPLE 2

Moving the accents out to the toms.

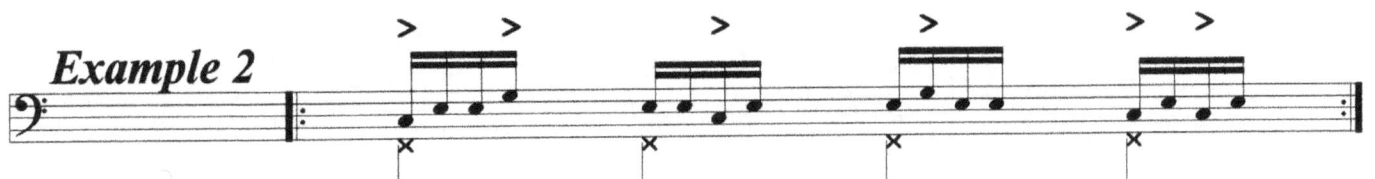

EXAMPLE 3

Moving the accents up to the cymbals with bass drum, now we are using all 4 limbs if you are still playing $^1/_4$ notes in the hi-hat foot.

EXAMPLE 4

Using example 1 but now doubling the un-accented notes, these doubles should be low in volume.

EXAMPLE 5

EXAMPLE 6

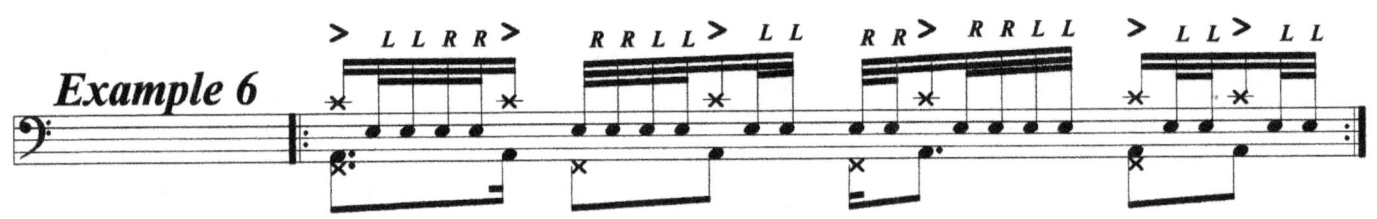

EXAMPLE 7

Starting to mix the previous ideas together to create new ones.

EXAMPLE 8

EXAMPLE 9

EXAMPLE 10

Watch out for the hi-hat opening (choke) on the (a of 1).

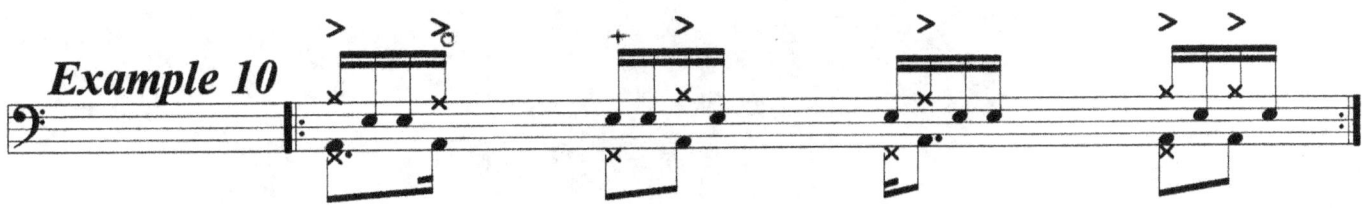

SOLO 1 GROOVE

You can use a groove of your own for the solo play-alongs if you wish. The ideas here are from the previous examples to create drum fills every 4 bars. However bars 20, 24, 28 and 32 have been left blank so you can use a pencil to write down some of your own ideas using previous examples. Notes in brackets mean ghost notes (to be played softly at a low volume) as seen in solo 1 groove below.

SOLO 1 GROOVE

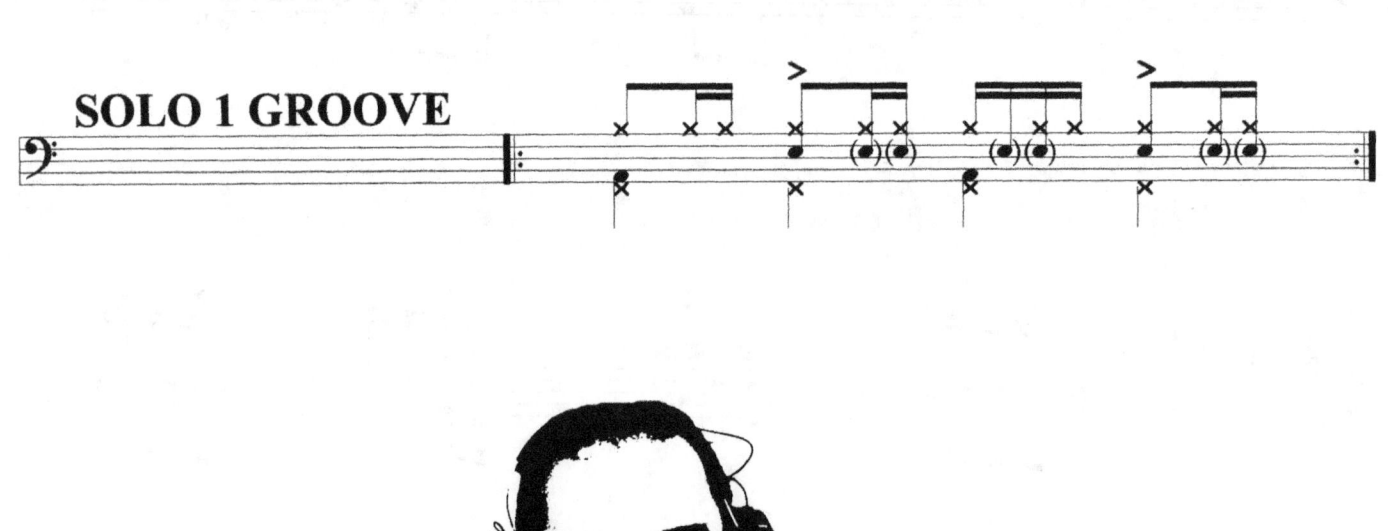

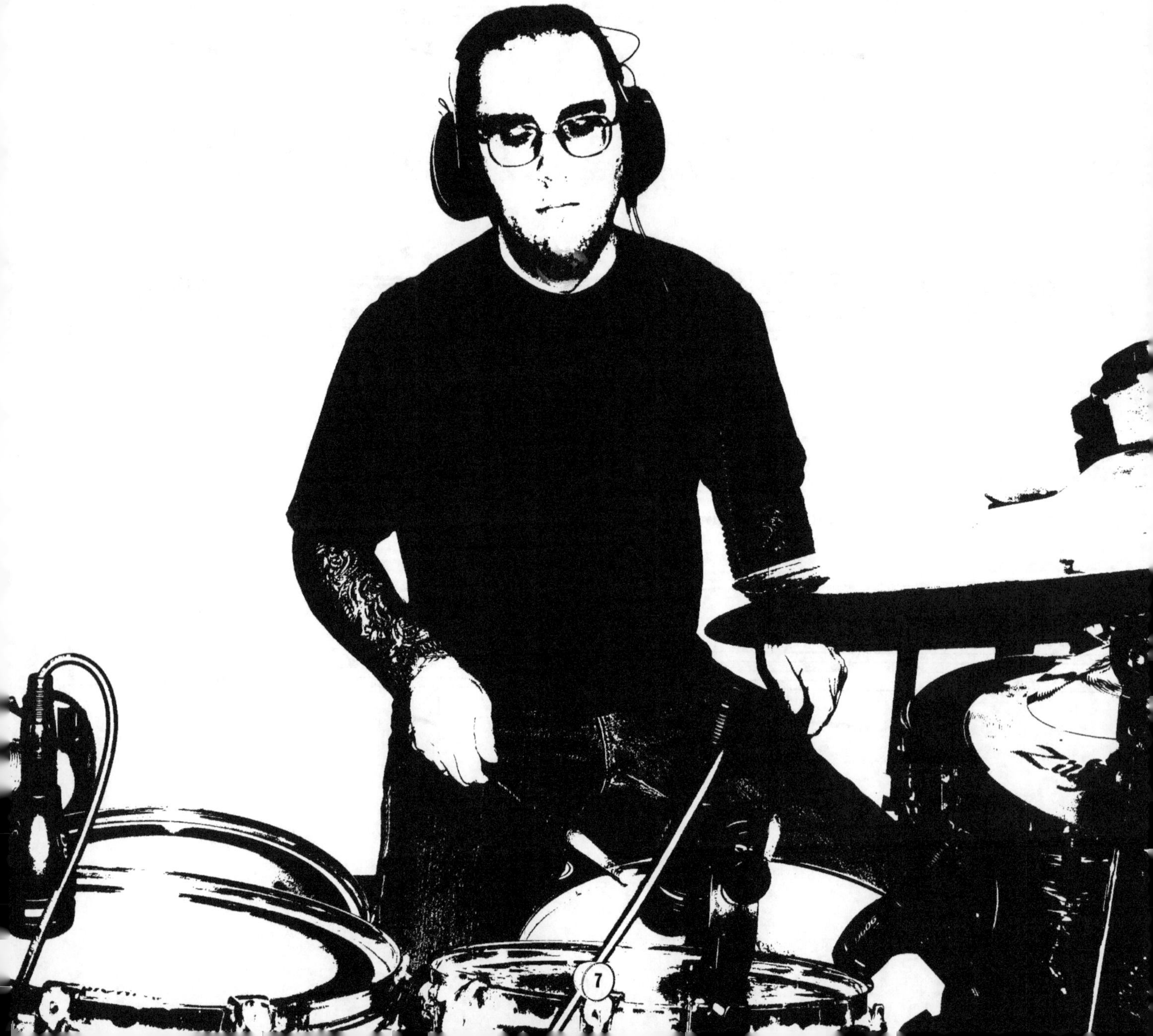

SOLO 1

EXAMPLE 11

The next 10 ideas have incorporated the phrase for different limbs or combining limbs whilst keeping time or a groove with the other limbs. Here the bass drum is playing the phrase while the other 3 limbs play a simple groove.

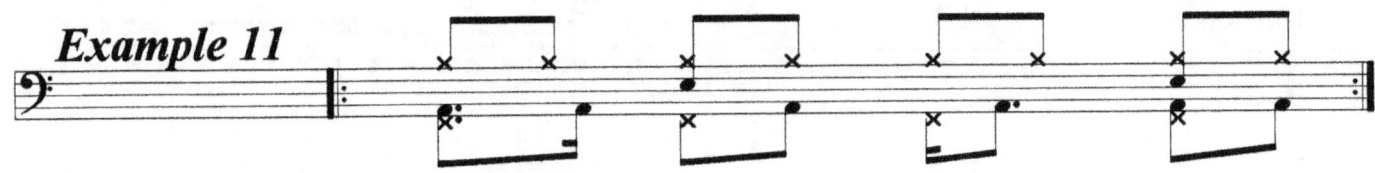

EXAMPLE 12

Here the snare drum is playing the phrase while the other 3 limbs are keeping time.

EXAMPLE 13

Here the ride cymbal is playing the phrase while the other 3 limbs are keeping time.

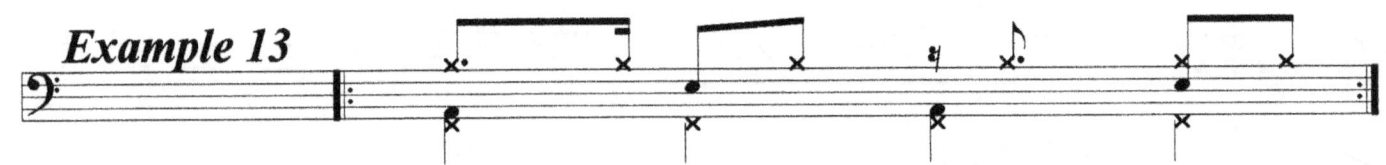

EXAMPLE 14

Here the hi-hat foot is playing the phrase. Some may understandably find this tricky to do, so remember to start slowly. Repetition is key, if you are to achieve your goal.

EXAMPLE 15

The phrase is now being played between bass drum and snare, starting with the bass.

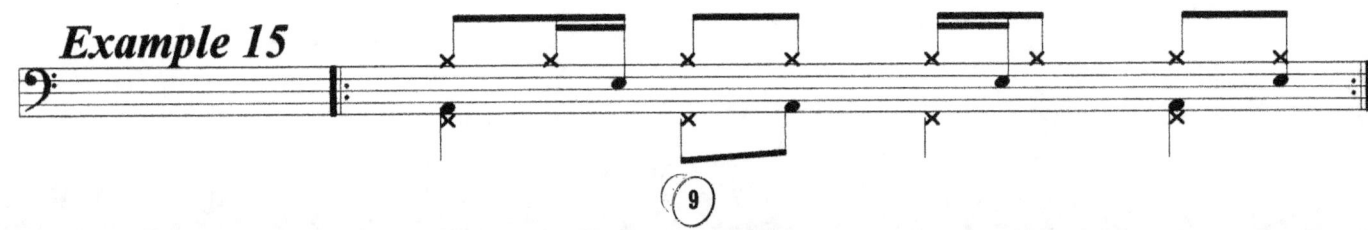

EXAMPLE 16

Same idea as the previous one but now starting with the snare drum.

EXAMPLE 17

This idea is using the bass drum and snare but orchestrating them more into a funk type groove. Try different ways of playing these groove ideas, for example playing the bell of the ride cymbal on the $1/4$ notes or accenting the upbeat 1/8 note (the &s) on the bell.

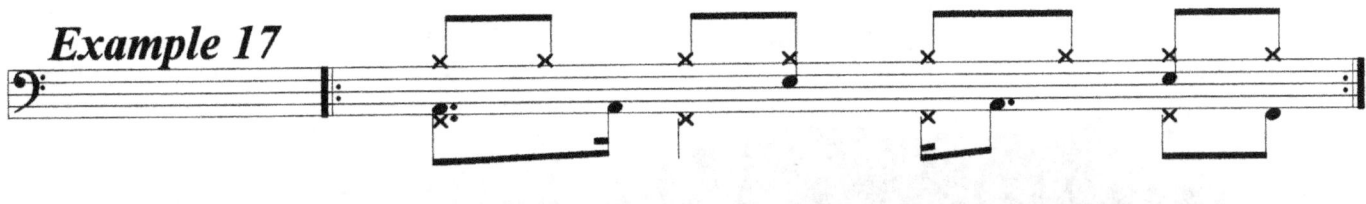

EXAMPLE 18

The next 3 ideas are just advancing this use of the phrase, experiment with these ideas and be creative. You don't have to play the snare on beat 2 all the time, for example you could use the 1st tom or the floor tom for beat 2 to give it a Latin flavour.

EXAMPLE 19

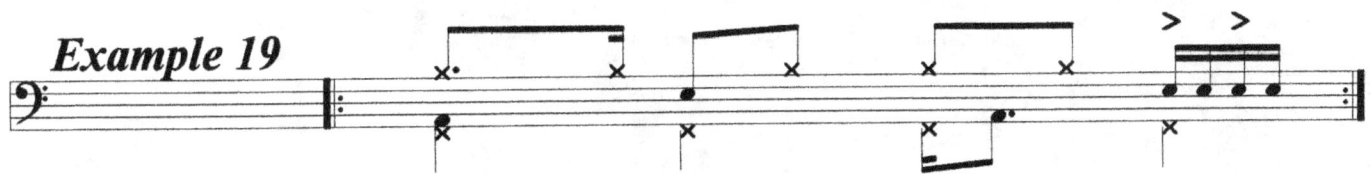

EXAMPLE 20

SOLO 2 GROOVE

The groove for solo 2 is using the phrase idea in the bass drum and adding some ghost notes and a double on the snare to create a funk type groove. The first drum fill in bar 4 is using a different sticking, bar 8 is using the single stroke roll and for bar 12 and 16 the phrase is moving round the drums and cymbals, not really a drum fill just implying the idea of a drum fill within a groove.

SOLO 2 GROOVE

SOLO 2

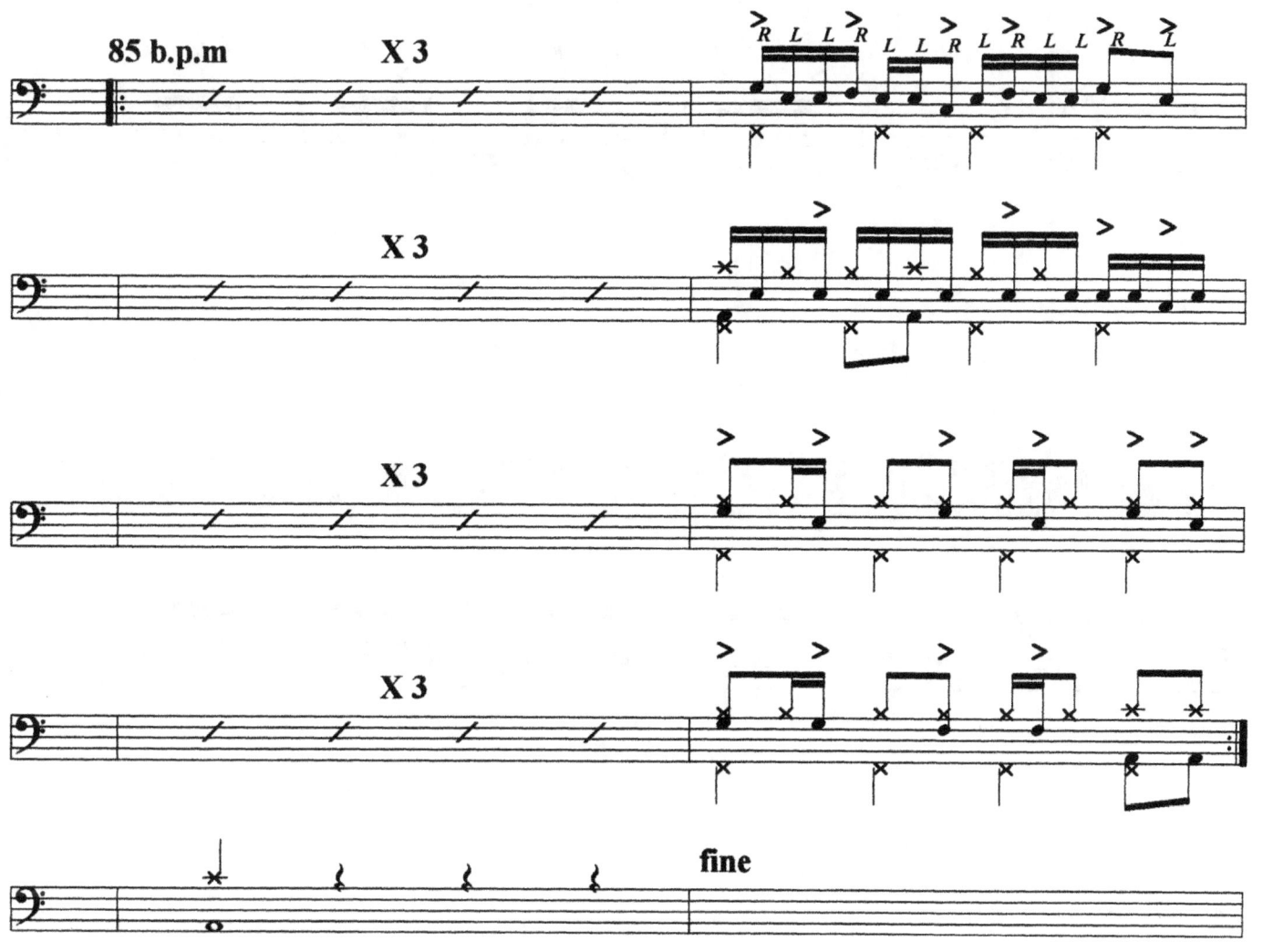

EXAMPLE 21

The next 10 ideas are using the mixed stickings that you played in bar 4 of solo 2. This will sound the same as example 1, it will however feel totally different to play against the $1/4$ note in the hi-hat foot and allows a lot of different possibilities and ideas to be created that you might not get using a single stroke roll.

EXAMPLE 22

EXAMPLE 23

Starting to develop the idea for use in a groove.

EXAMPLE 24

EXAMPLE 25

Basic idea for a groove which has many possibilities.

EXAMPLE 26

Developing some 4 way co-ordination to expand your ability to think outside of a written pattern.

EXAMPLE 27

This one has a nice funky bounce in the groove, good for use in a 4th or 8th bar idea instead of playing a drum fill every 4 or 8 bars which could interfere with the flow of a groove in a song.

EXAMPLE 28

The next 3 ideas are using the phrase as a type of punctuation idea, very common in a lot of styles of music.

EXAMPLE 29

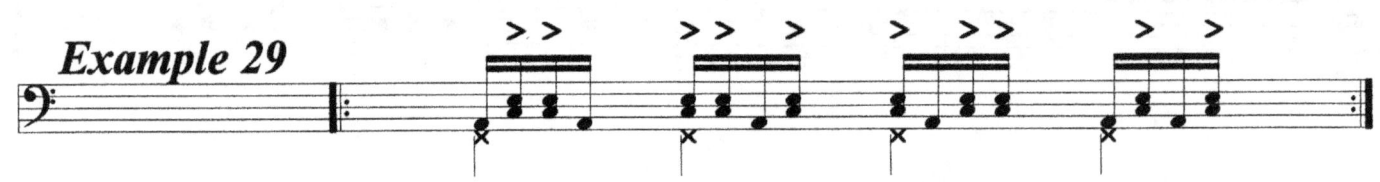

EXAMPLE 30

SOLO 3 GROOVE

The groove for solo 3 is a 2 bar pattern. Remember to play the ghost notes low in volume to create the right feel. You may need to spend more time practising examples 21 to 30 to play the drum fills that are written. With time and practice everything is playable.

SOLO 3 GROOVE 2 bar groove

SOLO 3

EXAMPLE 31

Bass and hi-hat foot are now playing the phrase through 16th notes whilst the hands are keeping time. If you are having trouble with this type of independence/co-ordination try just playing one limb first to the click and start to add bits a little at a time.

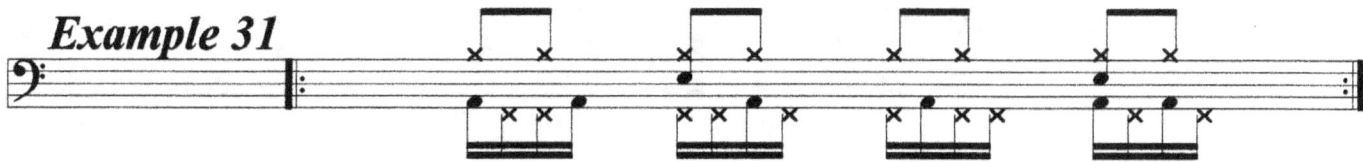

Example 31

EXAMPLE 32

Here is the reverse of the previous idea.

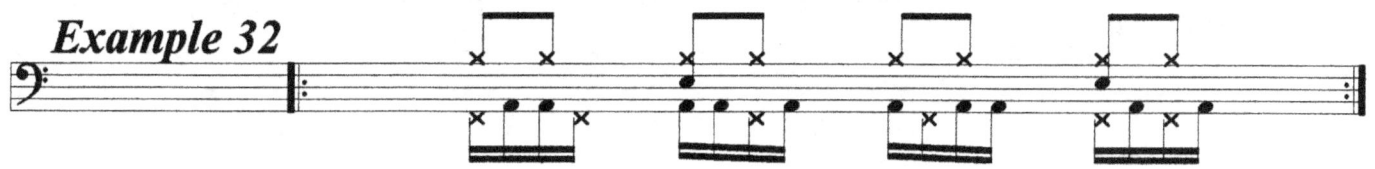

Example 32

EXAMPLE 33

The phrase is now played between bass and snare.

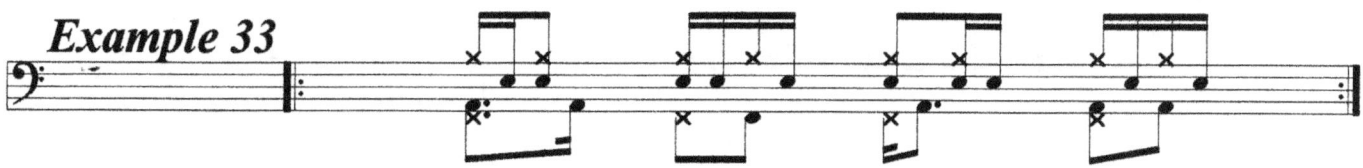

Example 33

EXAMPLE 34

Here is the reverse of the previous idea. Remember to move right or left hand around the kit with examples 31 to 34 to create some interesting ideas.

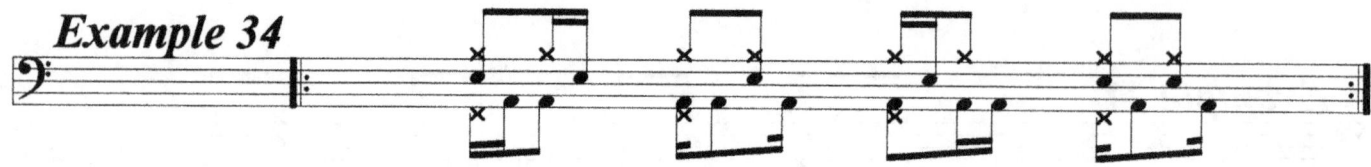

EXAMPLE 35

EXAMPLE 36

This idea is a little bit tricky at first but will set you up nicely for what's to come.

EXAMPLE 37

Example 37

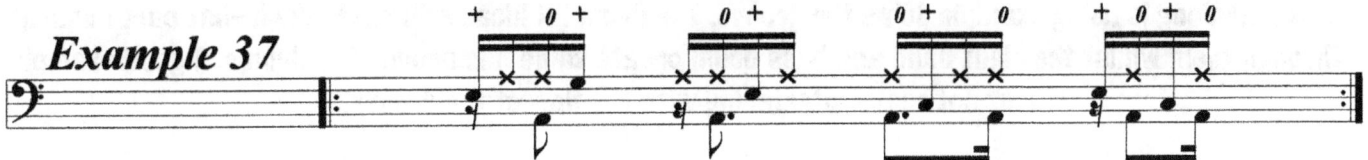

EXAMPLE 38

These 2 ideas are the parts you will need to learn in order to play example 40.

Example 38

EXAMPLE 39

Example 39

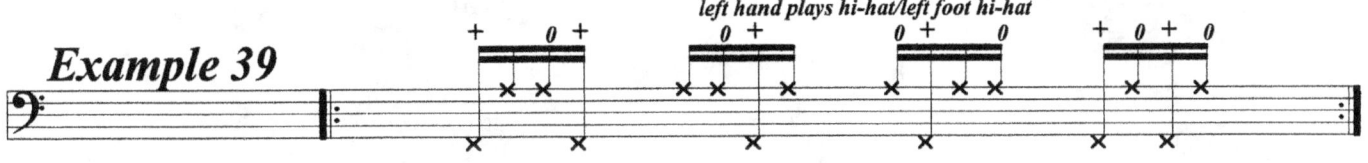

EXAMPLE 40

Example 40
examples 38 & 39 combined

SOLO 4 GROOVE

This playalong is using example 40 as the groove. The drum fill ideas still have the hi-hat part running through them whilst the right hand and bass drum create some fills around the drums. A good example of not really interfering with the flow of the groove.

SOLO 4 GROOVE

SOLO 4

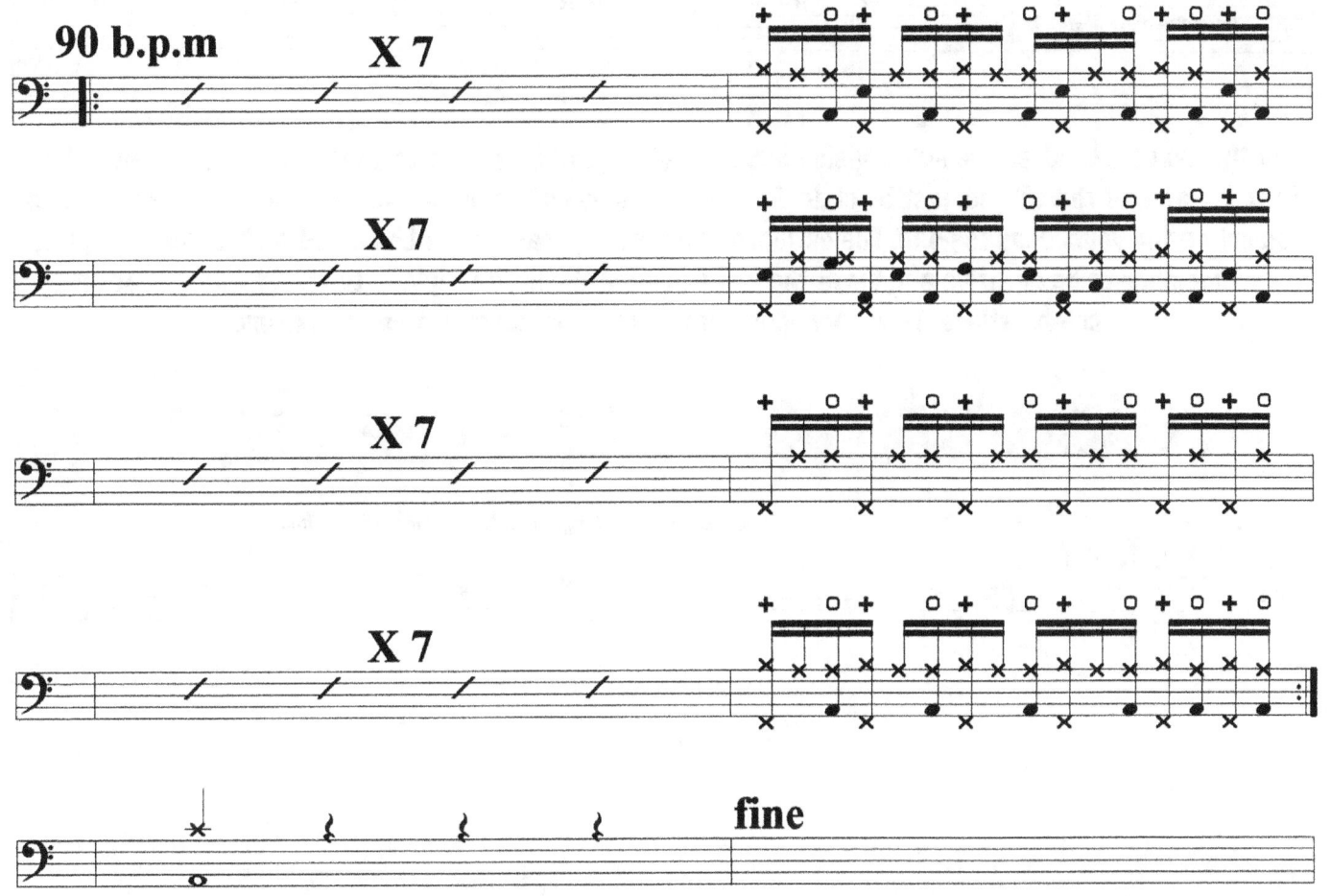

OSTINATO

Ostinato
for the following example's
left hand plays hi-hat

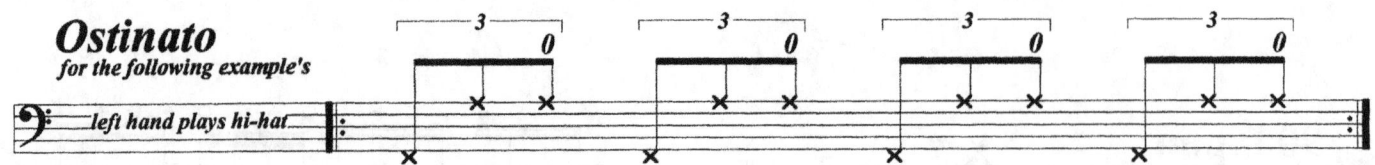

In the next lot of ideas the sub-division has been changed to 1/8 note triplets so now only using the first 12 notes of the phrase, just by changing the sub-division it can give you a whole different feel and direction for your ideas to go in. The ostinato (repetitive phrase) is to be played with all 10 examples, remember to be creative and move the ideas around the kit or replace the hand with a foot or combinations. There are many variations and permutations to explore.

EXAMPLE 41

Example 41

example's 41 - 48 right hand plays snare with ostinato

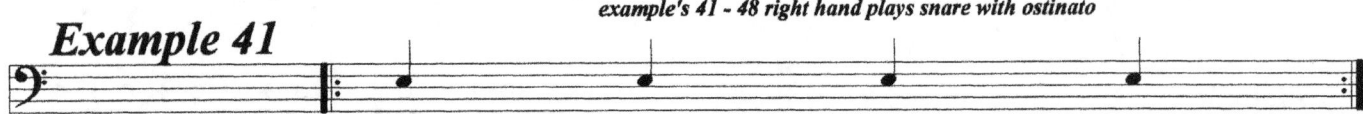

EXAMPLE 42

Example 42

EXAMPLE 43

Example 43

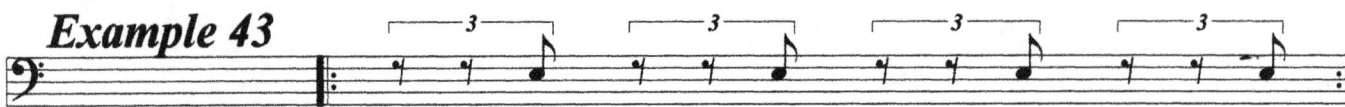

Example 44

Example 45

Example 46

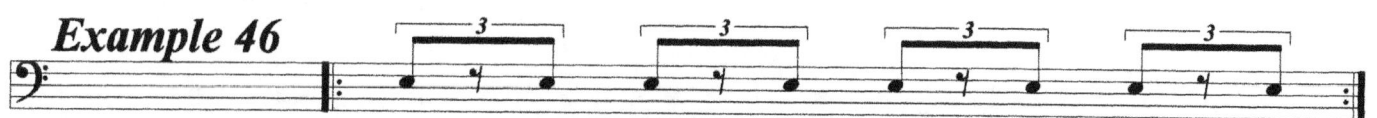

Example 47

EXAMPLE 48

EXAMPLE 49

The right hand is alternating between ride cymbal and snare to create a back beat on beats 2 and 4.

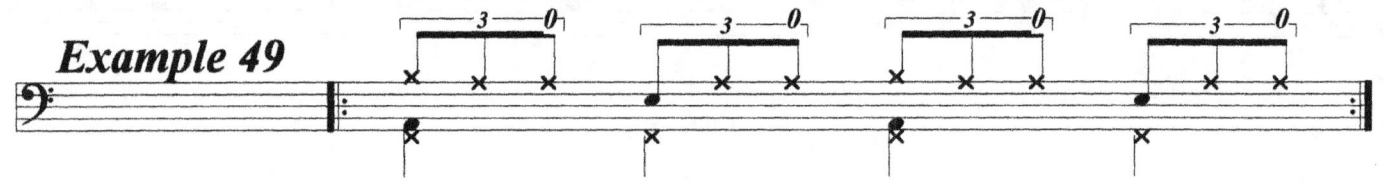

EXAMPLE 50

Same idea as the previous but playing the snare on beat 3 this time to give the groove a half time feel, watch out for the extra hit at the end on the ride cymbal.

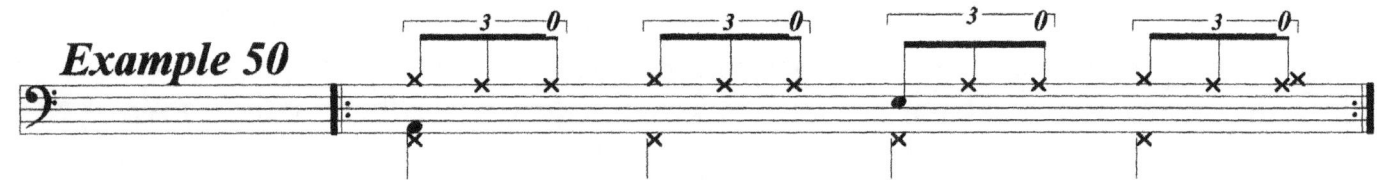

SOLO 5 GROOVE

The groove for solo 5 is a similar one to example 50 but the left hand is playing on the 1st tom to give it a different feel. The fill ideas all come from the previous examples whilst the left hand is still keeping the ostinato going with hi-hat foot. The phrase is being played between the hi-hat foot and left hand on 1st tom throughout this solo.

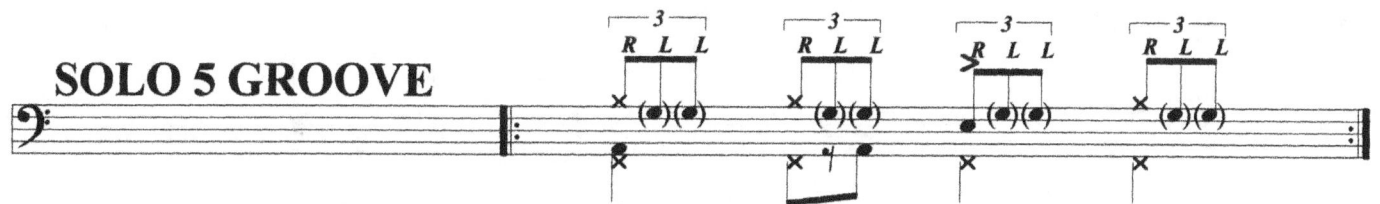

SOLO 5

50 BONUS IDEAS

The 50 bonus ideas are just some of the many ways in which I have developed this phrase or any other phrase that I am working on. There are far too many permutations and orchestrations to fit into one book, so here are 50 bonus ideas for advancing this common phrase which many drummers use or develop into something else.

no.1

These next few ideas you may recognise from solo 3 bar 24, this shows you how you can develop one idea by adding notes or replacing a hand with a foot. Let's start with moving the phrase down the toms and back up the toms. Remember with all these patterns to start slowly with click at 60 b.p.m and hi-hat foot on the $\frac{1}{4}$ notes.

no.2

The first left hand of each group of 3 is now replaced with the bass drum.

no.3

Now double the left hand of each group of 3 on the snare, explore the idea of not doubling every time, be inventive.

no.4

It is the bass drum now that is doubling to create the 32nd note while the hands play 16th notes.

no.5

The bass drum and the snare are both being played as doubles now to create this 16th/32nd note phrase.

no.6

The next few ideas are developing the phrase which is being played between bass drum and the right hand and orchestrated around the kit. One of a thousand orchestrations.

no.7

Now add the off beat 32nd note with the left hand through the same pattern.

no.8

For double bass pedal users. However if you have a fast right foot or want to develop speed in your right foot then just use the one foot pedal, you will only be able to get this to a certain speed with one foot so you may want to eventually invest in a double pedal.

no.9

Now add the off beat 32nd note with the left hand through the same pattern.

no.10

Same idea as the previous one but a different orchestration.

no.11

no.12

no.13

no.14

Similar idea as before but starting with the hands and stopping on beat 4 to punctuate the phrase.

no.15

PHRASE PERMUTATIONS

Starting the phrase on the bass drum it is easy to apply some permutations, all we do is start the next phrase a 16th note earlier; so you take the last 16th note and place it at the front of the next phrase until it all returns to where you started from. Lots of ideas out of one simple permutation rule and don't forget to orchestrate these ideas all over the kit. There is a lot of mileage in using this rule. Be creative.

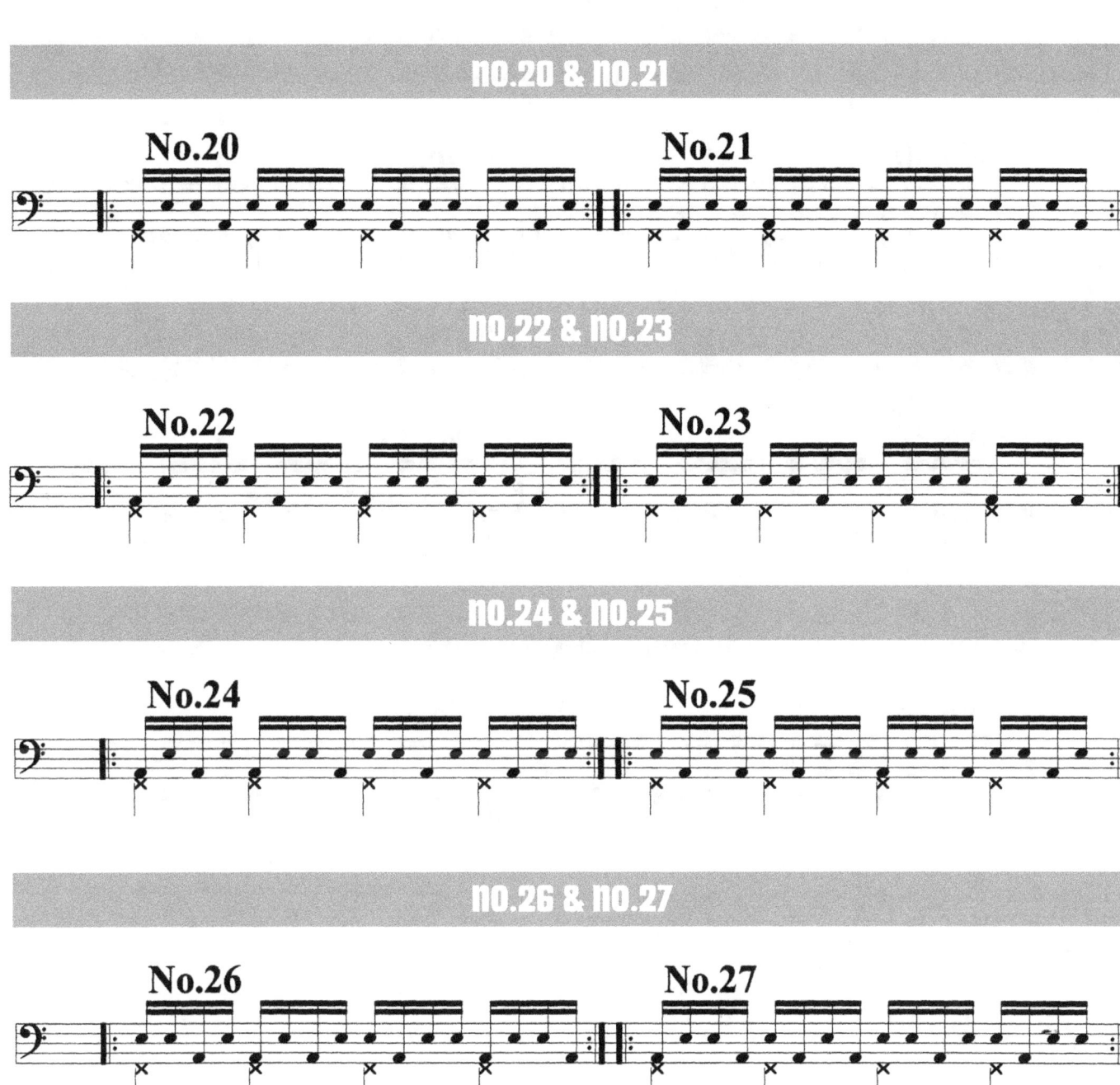

No.28 & 29

No.30 & 31

No.32 & No.33

No.34 & No.35

4 IDEAS TO APPLY THE PREVIOUS PATTERNS TO

no. 36

using No.25 and applying it to 32nd notes

No.36

no. 37

using No.35 and applying it to a groove

No.37

no. 38

using No.20 and applying it to a fill, use both hands together for power across the fill

No.38
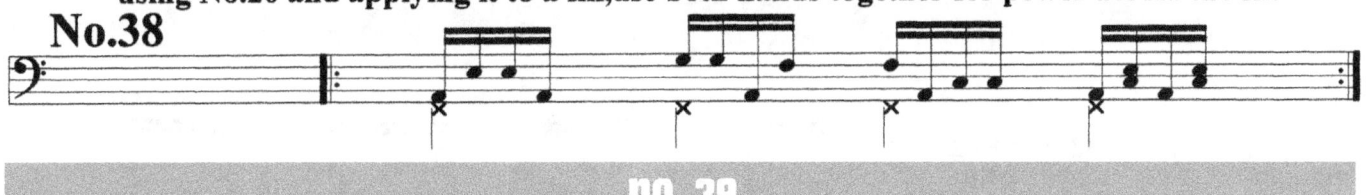

no. 39

using No.33 between bass and ride and placing a back beat on 2 and 4

No.39

GROOVE IDEAS

The next 5 groove ideas all have the rhythmic phrase within them, with practice and imagination you can create your own interesting grooves.

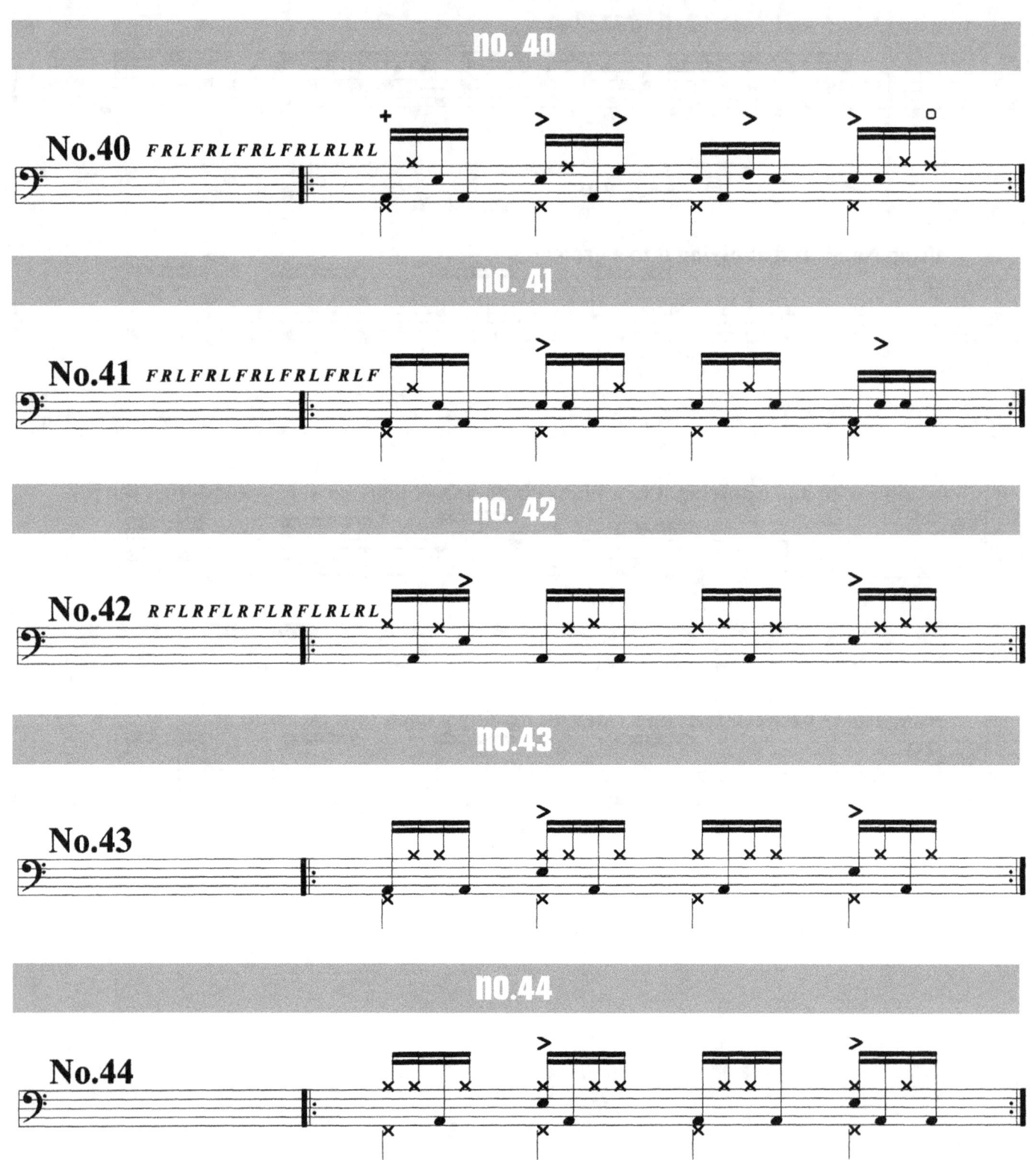

METRIC MODULATION IDEAS

Metric modulation is a rhythmic illusion, in other words, the altering of a conventional pattern in order to persuade the listener that the tempo and/or time signature has momentarily changed.

Superimposing one rhythm on top of an existing one can be a useful tool for creating tension and excitement in the correct musical setting. VERY COOL.

These next ideas have two 16th notes then a 16th note rest repeated on the ride cymbal across 3 bars, you should by now see that the 16th note rest is actually from the first three $\frac{1}{4}$ notes of the rhythmic phrase but without the 4 and the & of 4 at the start of this book.

You may find it easier to count these grooves in $\frac{3}{4}$ time first and when you are comfortable with this then all you have to do is change the $\frac{3}{4}$ count to 4/4 count, remember to play the hi-hat foot on the $\frac{1}{4}$ notes throughout these grooves to ground your counting and internal clock to know where the 1 is and also to give your fellow musicians and the listener a time reference.

NO. 45 & NO. 46

The bass drum and snare drum have been placed on the second partial of each group of two 16th notes that you're playing on the ride cymbal, this gives the listener the illusion that you are playing a shuffle groove in a new tempo.

Take any 3 beat section to create a $\frac{3}{4}$ time signature, or you could also take a 5 beat section to create a 5/4 time signature and so on with 6's, 7's and 9's etc.

no. 47 & no. 48

This groove is not so much a metric modulation because the back beat remains on 2 and 4, a common ride pattern either played across 3 bars or broken up into sections. Experiment.

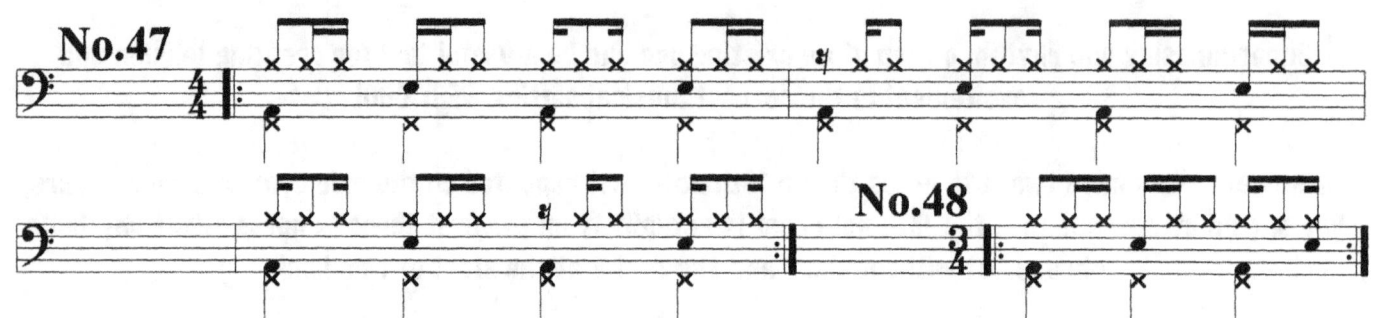

no. 49 & no. 50

This groove has the bass drum and snare placed where the 16th note rest would be.

These are all challenging ways of advancing the rhythmic phrase and will take time to perfect, try not to get frustrated, little and often is the key so take your time and choose the things that you feel will benefit your playing the most.

USE FOR YOUR OWN IDEAS

USE FOR YOUR OWN IDEAS

www.ingramcontent.com/pod-product-compliance
Lightning Source LLC
Chambersburg PA
CBHW081421300426
44110CB00017BA/2343